Groundhogs

Woodchucks, Marmots, and Whistle Pigs

by Adele D. Richardson

Consultant:
Kenneth B. Armitage
Baumgartner Professor Emeritus
The University of Kansas

Bridgestone Books
an imprint of Capstone Press
Mankato, Minnesota

Bridgestone Books are published by Capstone Press
151 Good Counsel Drive, P.O. Box 669, Mankato, Minnesota 56002
http://www.capstone-press.com

Library of Congress Cataloging-in-Publication Data
Richardson, Adele, 1966–
    Groundhogs: woodchucks, marmots, and whistle pigs/by Adele D. Richardson.
    p.cm.—(Wild world of animals)
    Summary: An introduction to the physical characteristics, behavior, habitat, and life
cycle of groundhogs, rodents that may hibernate for six months during the winter.
    Includes bibliographical references (p. 24) and index.
    ISBN 0-7368-1397-7 (hardcover)
    1. Woodchuck—Juvenile literature. 2. Marmots—Juvenile literature. [1. Woodchuck.
2. Marmots.] I. Title. II. Series.
QL737.R68 R53 2003
599.36'6—dc21   2002000081

Editorial Credits
Heather Adamson, editor; Karen Risch, product planning editor; Linda Clavel, designer;
    Anne McMullen, interior illustrator; Kelly Garvin, photo researcher

Photo Credits
Eda Rogers, 6
Jesse M. Harris, 18
Joe McDonald, cover, 1, 4, 10
Lynn Charles (Delaware), 14, 20
Norman Owen Tomalin/Bruce Coleman Inc., 8
Tom Boyden, 16
Visions of Nature (texture), 2, 3, 4, 6, 10, 12, 20, 22, 23, 24

1 2 3 4 5 6 07 06 05 04 03 02

Table of Contents

ear

eye

tail

claws

FUN FACTS

Groundhogs are also called woodchucks, marmots, and whistle pigs.

Groundhogs

Groundhogs have thick bodies and short legs. They have small ears and large, black eyes. Groundhogs are covered with fur. Their fur is grizzled brown. They usually grow to about 20 inches (50 centimeters) long. They weigh about 9 pounds (4 kilograms).

grizzled
lighter colors mixed through dark hair or fur

Groundhogs can run at speeds up to 10 miles (16 kilometers) per hour.

Groundhogs Are Mammals

Groundhogs are mammals. They are warm-blooded. They have a backbone and hair. Female mammals feed milk to their young. Groundhogs can swim and climb trees like many other mammals. Groundhogs are rodents like mice and beavers are.

rodent
a mammal with large, sharp front teeth used for gnawing

A Groundhog's Habitat

Groundhogs live across the eastern United States and southern Canada. They dig burrows. Groundhog burrows are near food sources. Most burrows are on the edges of forests or in open fields.

habitat
the place where an animal lives

FUN FACTS

A groundhog's front teeth grow throughout its entire life.

What Do Groundhogs Eat?

Groundhogs eat mostly plants like clover, grass, and wildflowers. They sometimes eat insects. They may eat tree bark or branches if they are very hungry. Groundhogs have four large front teeth for biting plants. They also have flat teeth for chewing.

FUN FACTS ! Groundhogs spend a lot of time in their burrows in summer. They go underground to keep cool.

12

Hibernation

Groundhogs hibernate in their burrows. They prepare by eating large amounts of food. Groundhogs go in their burrows in the fall. They block all the openings with dirt. Groundhogs hibernate for about four months. They come out when the weather gets warm.

hibernate
to spend winter in a deep, sleeplike condition

13

Mating and Birth

Males search for females to mate with after hibernating. Females give birth to young about a month later. Three to five young groundhogs make up a litter. They are born in the burrow. Female groundhogs take care of the litter by themselves.

Groundhog Pups

Young groundhogs are called pups or kits. Pups are born blind. They have no fur. The pups are about 4 inches (10 centimeters) long and weigh 1 ounce (28 grams). Their mothers feed them milk for about six weeks. Groundhogs may live 4 to 6 years.

Predators

Groundhogs must watch for predators. Wolves, foxes, coyotes, and eagles hunt groundhogs. Groundhogs usually escape into their burrows. They warn others by making a sound like a whistle. Groundhogs may grind their teeth to scare predators.

whistle
an instrument that makes a high, loud sound

The groundhog is the only animal to have a holiday named after it. February 2 is Groundhog Day in the United States. People watch the groundhog come out of its burrow. People believe that winter will soon be over if the groundhog does not see its shadow.

20

Groundhogs and People

Many farmers think groundhogs are pests. Groundhogs dig in fields. They eat farm crops like corn and cabbage. Groundhogs can help farmers too. Snakes and foxes make homes in deserted groundhog burrows. They eat rats and mice that can harm crops.

Hands On: Digging Race

Digging a burrow is easy for groundhogs. Their long, curved claws are perfect for digging into the ground. Try this game with some friends.

What You Need

Two or more friends
A watch or minute timer
Plastic forks
A sandbox or area of dirt
A ruler

What You Do

1. One person must be the timekeeper. The others will be diggers. Each digger needs a plastic fork and a place to dig.
2. The timekeeper says, "Go!" The diggers start digging holes with their forks. After one minute, the timekeeper says, "Stop!"
3. Use the ruler to see who dug the deepest hole. That person is the winning groundhog. Fill the holes back in with dirt. Try the game again.

A groundhog's claws sink easily into dirt like the sharp points of the plastic forks. Groundhogs can dig very fast. In one day, they can dig a hole 5 feet (1.5 meters) long and 4 inches (10 centimeters) wide.

Words to Know

burrow (BUR-oh)—a tunnel or hole in the ground where an animal lives

litter (LIT-ur)—a group of animals born at the same time to the same mother

mammal (MAM-uhl)—a warm-blooded animal with hair that has a backbone and feeds milk to its young

mate (MATE)—to join together to produce young

predator (PRED-uh-tur)—an animal that hunts and eats other animals

rodent (ROHD-uhnt)—a mammal with large, sharp front teeth used for gnawing

warm-blooded (warm-BLUHD-id)—an animal that does not use its surroundings to control its body temperature

Read More

Dingwall, Laima. *Woodchucks.* Nature's Children. Danbury, Conn.: Grolier Books, 1999.

Kalman, Bobbie. *What is a Rodent?* The Science of Living Things. New York: Crabtree Publishing Company, 2000.

Internet Sites

Canadian Wildlife Service—Hinterland's Who's Who—Woodchuck
http://www.cws-scf.ec.gc.ca/hww-fap/woodchuc/woodchuc.html

Dunkirk Dave's Groundhog Haven!
http://www.dunkirkdave.org/day.html

Index